# How Movies Are Made

Text    Gwen Cherrell
Design  Eddie Poulton

## Contents

Facts On File
New York • Oxford

# History

In the 1870s in California Edward Muybridge set up twenty-four cameras alongside a race track. He attached threads to the shutters of each camera and stretched them across the track. He then sent a horse galloping past the cameras. As it did so, it broke the threads and thereby photographed itself. When Muybridge developed the images from the separate plates of his camera and printed them, he had a series of photographs showing continuous motion.

In Europe, other pioneers were also working on motion pictures. During the 1880s in England William Friese-Green was working on his motion-picture camera, and in America George Eastman invented the celluloid roll film. In the 1890s in France the Lumière brothers invented a "claw" mechanism with hooks which caught the film by the perforations along its edges and pulled each frame into position, working like a shuttle on a sewing machine. Clear images were projected on to a screen for the first time by Robert Paul in England and by Woodville Latham in America in 1895.

The first film studio was built for the Thomas A. Edison company in New Jersey in 1893. Painted black inside and out and known as the "Black Maria," the Kinetographic Theater had a revolving base which allowed action to be photographed all day by following the sun. To exhibit the pictures, Edison invented the Kinetoscope, but audiences were obliged to peer into it, one person at a time. After 1894, pictures were projected on to a screen.

At first, all moving pictures were made without sound. Then in 1906 Lee de Forest invented the audion tube by means of which, using photographs of sound waves obtained via electronic valves, he was able to amplify sounds picked up by a microphone. For twenty years his invention was ignored, and only silent movies were produced. The "talkies" arrived in 1927. By the 1930s, the combination of sight and sound had lost its novelty. Major studio companies gave the industry a boost by exploiting the star system. A typical program of the time would include a feature film (90 mins), second feature (60 mins), newsreel (10 mins), cartoon, "interest" or comedy short (10 mins), and trailer of forthcoming attractions (3 mins), with interval (7 mins)—a total of three hours.

Lilian Gish, whose career began in 1912 and continued into the 1980s, is seen on the set of *La Bohème* (1926). Gish appeared in many classic silent films for the great director D.W. Griffith, including his masterpiece *The Birth of a Nation* (1915). Griffith was the first film-maker to produce the close-up and long shot for narrative use, to move the camera alongside the action, and to use editing techniques such as cross-cuts.

Also seen are Irving Thalberg who, as Executive Producer at MGM studios in Hollywood in the 1930s, created a distinctive style with a team of great stars: King Vidor (middle) who directed pictures for forty years; and cameraman Hendrick Sartov. Once Griffith's special effects man, Sartov was the inventor of the soft focus lens.

Charlie Chaplin faces Ford Sterling in *Between Showers* (1914), the fourth of thirty-five films which Chaplin made during his first year in the industry. As writer, producer, director and actor of his own films, Chaplin holds a unique position in movie history.

Below. Still from *The Seven Samurai* (1954), showing leading Japanese actor Toshiro Mifune in foreground. The film was directed by Akira Kurasawa, whose earlier work *Rashomon* had won first prize at the 1951 Venice Film Festival and introduced Japanese films to the West. Kurasawa's powerful interpretation of the Samurai code of chivalry and idealism influenced Hollywood director John Sturges, who created a "Western" version, *The Magnificent Seven* (1960), set in Mexico.

Kinemacolor had been invented in 1906 by the British pioneer G. A. Smith, who used color filters. The first successful color negatives were patented by Herbert Kalmus in 1931. Trick photography was introduced in Paris in 1900, by Georges Méliès, to create fantasy films. In 1933 the special effects created in Hollywood for *King Kong* set the pace for modern **opticals**. Wide-screen techniques were first used in France by Abel Gance in 1927. They were revived by Hollywood in the 1950s and were expanded through the Canadian IMAX system in the 1970s. The 1980s saw significant advances in film laboratory techniques. Rank Film Laboratories designed a system for printing and processing the entire length of a feature film (13,000ft) as a single roll. This method produces show-copy quality for release printing.

# Pre-production: The Flow Chart

To make an independent feature film, a production company is formed. It requires the skills of ten or more different departments of artists, technicians and craftsmen. The work schedule is divided into three periods: pre-production, production (the shoot) and post-production. It takes around fifty weeks to complete, depending on the kind of film that is being made—large cast with lavish sets or small cast shot on location.

What is a feature film? It is a movie which runs for ninety minutes or more and is regarded as being the principal attraction at the movie theater. It begins with an idea.

## STAGE ONE: PRE-PRODUCTION

### CONCEPT
Written in the form of a book, a story or on a single sheet of paper. An **option** to make a movie based on the idea is purchased by the Producer.

### SCREENWRITER
is assigned to supply a "treatment" of the idea. This is a summary of the story, giving brief descriptions of the characters and principal sequences around which the plot will be developed.

### RESEARCH
Subject matter is examined for accuracy.

### SCREENWRITER
Writes a Full Script: a detailed narrative with dialog. Each scene is numbered in chronological order and is defined "interior" or "exterior".

### FINANCIAL BACKING
is sought from the Distribution Companies and/or from outside the film industry as speculative investment through banks.

### SCRIPT BREAKDOWN
The analysis of a film script, determining all expenses for budget proposals, is prepared by Producer and Director.

### FINANCIAL BACKING
is secured.

### BUDGET BREAKDOWN
**FEES**
Producer, Director, actors, composer, musicians, heads of departments and consultants (casting and publicity).

**SALARIES**
Production staff, technical and crafts staff.

**RENTALS**
Technical equipment—camera, lighting, sound, location projector (editing) and general film supplies; their vehicles.

Editing room and equipment.

Art Department—costumes, wigs, props and set dressings.

Transportation vehicles. Animals.

**EXPENSES**
Location: site-scouting, permissions and preparation, accommodation and daily catering, location telephones, travelling and trailers, First Aid nurse.

Laboratory: stock film (processed and printed), sound transfer (printed and coded), opticals and titles **CRI** (color), sound effects.

Editorial: dailies—prints and transportation, negative cutter, effects editor.

Music: copyrights.

Also: special effects, designer creations, contributions to social security and pension funds, insurance cover, promotional and advertising costs.

### PRINCIPAL ACTORS
### MUSIC COMPOSER
### HEADS OF DEPARTMENTS
are contracted.

## STAGE TWO: SHOOTING

### SHOOTING SCHEDULE

is drawn up. A back-up schedule is also prepared to prevent interruption of work thru illness, bad weather, mechanical/technical problems.

### PRODUCTION PERIOD

Shooting takes place creating film footage from which the movie will be manufactured. Includes blocking (marking) positions and movements of cameras, crews and cast, before photographing every set-up.

## STAGE THREE: POST-PRODUCTION

### POST PRODUCTION

Laboratory processing, begun during shooting, continues.

### EDITING

Picture Editor assembles the film as it has been shot.

### ROUGH CUT

First complete assemblage of material, with dialog only.

### FINE CUT

The final version, to which music, sound, special effects and titles are added.

### LABORATORIES

Final laboratory work for camera-negative cutting and printing.

### MARKETING

Distributing company promotes the finished package.

# Film Unit Structure

"Put it on paper!"

During pre-production, the Producer, Director and Production Manager, working together, select the key members of the unit to be their Heads of Departments. These are the Director of Photography (sometimes known as Lighting Cameraman or Cinematographer), Art Director, Sound Mixer and Editor. It is usual for them to assemble their own crews.

The Producer brings in the Script Supervisor (also known as Continuity) and the First (Assistant Director) who nominates the Second and Third Assistant Directors.

With so many departments using a scattered work force, up-to-date information from each department is vital. Work-in-progress is charted and circulated to all sections. During **shooting**, there are two central reference sheets. The first is the Schedule. For this, the shooting script is broken down into a timetable of events for each

## PRODUCER
Head of film production who co-ordinates and supervises all artistic aspects of the production.

### PRODUCTION STAFF

### ASSOCIATE PRODUCER
Second-in-command.

### PRODUCTION SUPERVISOR
works with
### PRODUCTION MANAGER
Negotiate business deals with the crews. Administrate the day-to-day details of the production.

### PRODUCTION CO-ORDINATOR
From the Production Office back at base s/he keeps the Unit informed of work in progress.

### PRODUCER'S ASSISTANT
Personal Secretary to the Producer.

### LOCATION MANAGER
Administrates location shooting, from site-finding to eventual payment of the account for use of the site.

### PRODUCTION ACCOUNTANT
Resident paymaster and keeper of the books.

### UNIT PUBLICITY OFFICE

### PUBLICIST
Assembles and releases information to the media. Arranges interviews with the cast.

### PUBLICITY ASSISTANT
Composes captions for still photography.

### STILLS PHOTOGRAPHER
Takes publicity shots of cast and of work on the set.

## DIRECTOR
The artistic interpreter of the screenplay (also referred to as the script).

### SCREEN WRITER
Writes the screenplay.

### COMPOSER
Writes the theme music, mood music, background music.

### CONDUCTOR
### MUSICIANS
Record the score.

### SCRIPT SUPERVISOR
Keeps continuity references of all details during takes. Works closely with the Director.

### FIRST ASSISTANT DIRECTOR
Manages the floor and organizes cast and crews. Assists the Director in the direction of extras in crowd scenes. Is responsible for production (shooting) paperwork.

### SECOND ASSISTANT
Is the liaison between the floor and the Production Office, and between the floor and the cast.

### THIRD ASSISTANT
**Go-fer** for the Second Assistant.

### SECOND UNIT

### DIRECTOR
On location, shoots background shots, stunt shots and stunt doubles.

### CAMERA, SOUND, LIGHTING
Second unit crew.

### CAMERA DEPARTMENT

### DIRECTOR OF PHOTOGRAPHY (DP)
Head of department. Shoots the picture.

### CAMERA OPERATOR
Operates the machinery.

### FIRST ASSISTANT CAMERAMAN (FOCUS PULLER)
Sets up the camera with appropriate lens and filters. Sets the focus. Is responsible for camera maintenance.

### SECOND ASSISTANT CAMERAMAN (CLAPPER LOADER)
In charge of the slate and the camera paper work. Loads the camera magazine.

day of the week from the beginning of shooting until its ending; it includes travelling and rest days.

The Schedule reveals precisely what is being shot, where and when. Although in the shooting script the scenes are numbered in story (i.e. chronological) order, the script is not shot in story order. All scenes concerned with each individual set are completed before the unit goes on to the next (scheduled) set. The picture is shot on a sound-stage (inside the studio), on the lot (in the studio grounds) or on location (indoors or outdoors elsewhere).

The second central reference sheet is the Daily Call Sheet. It is put together, usually by the Second Assistant Director, around five o'clock each day. It is a listing of the following day's work. It contains the time of the **unit call**, giving set locations, the scenes by number, and whether they are interior or exterior, day or night. This is followed by the cast list of names, characters, dressing room numbers; the time of arrival for each of them at the studio, the make-up call, and the time required on the set. The Art Department list states which props will be required, and which special effects will be needed. If overtime working has been agreed, the Call Sheet will be marked "extended day".

## ART DEPARTMENT

### PRODUCTION DESIGNER
Head of department. Creates the overall design and determines the "look" of the film.

### ART DIRECTOR
Responsible for planning and creating the set designs.

### COSTUME DESIGNER
Creates the original designs. Supervises the purchasing of all costumes.

### SET DECORATOR
Selects and arranges set dressings and props as designed.

### PROPERTY MASTER
In charge of maintenance of all props. Keeps the props inventory.

### SET DRESSER
Assistant to property department.

### PROPERTY MAKER
Designs and constructs specially required props.

### GREENSMAN
Selects and maintains all greenery and flowers on the set.

### CONSTRUCTION MANAGER
Head carpenter. Supervises all construction work, including scaffolding.

### CONSTRUCTION CREW
Carpenters, painters, paper hangers, plasterers, welders, etc.

### MAKE-UP DESIGNER
Creates special make-ups. Organizes make-up artists. Supervises all make-ups. In charge of all make-up personnel.

### MAKE-UP ARTIST
Reproduces make-up designs. Assists make-up designer.

### HAIRDRESSER/STYLIST
Designs special styles. In charge of wigs and wig-dressing, toupeés (hair-pieces), moustaches, etc.

### WARDROBE
Handles the costumes on the set and is responsible for their care and maintenance. Dressers assist the actors.

## LIGHTING

### GAFFER
Head of department. Takes his orders from the Director of Photography.

### BEST BOY
Chief electrician. Reports to the Gaffer.

### LIGHTING CREW
Move and maintain equipment.

## GRIPS

### KEY GRIP
Supervises all grip crews. Answerable to the Director of Photography. Assists camera crew.

## SOUND

### SOUND MIXER
Head of department. Supervises all sound levels during shooting and post-production editing.

### RECORDIST
Assists Sound Mixer. Responsible for the choice and maintenance of equipment.

### BOOM OPERATOR
Handles the microphones.

### SOUND MAINTENANCE
Electrical engineer.

## EDITING

### EDITOR
Head of department. Cuts the film material. Makes the decisions (in conjunction with the Producer and the Director).

### PICTURE OR ASSISTANT EDITOR
Makes the cuts.

### SOUND EDITOR
Works with the Mixer. Cuts the sound.

### DUBBING EDITOR
Mixes the dialog, music, and sound effects tracks on to one track.

### DIALOG, SOUND EFFECTS, MUSIC
Specialist sound editors.

### LABORATORIES
Process film negative. Transfer tape sound to optical track and produce married print.

### OPTICAL HOUSE
Creates optical effects and titles.

# The Set

Any area in which action is shot is referred to as the Set. The Production Designer determines the "look" of the movie: s/he covers all visual aspects of the work. It is the job of the Art Director to interpret, in practical terms, the Director's and the Production Designer's vision of the script through the sets.

Using his knowledge of art history, architecture and interior design, and his ability to draw, design, use paint and create blue-prints, the Art Director first charts the facts and figures on how to achieve his aim. The artwork itself begins with painted drawings of every set which has to be constructed. These will be made to the Director's specifications. They might be for **wild walls**, for example, to allow camera and lights to move in and out. Using his knowledge of color photography, the Art Director selects the coloring for the set dressings, interior and exterior. These are assembled from outside hire companies by the Set Decorator, or they are made from materials which are specially

purchased under his or her supervision.

The Property Master runs the Property Department, which includes all kinds of talents such as that of the Greensman who provides trees and makes gardens. S/he keeps an inventory of all props used in the production and is responsible for their care and maintenance. Props, with the help of a Prop Maker and a Model Builder, is expected to make, fake or supply almost anything which is in use on the set. And, what is more, to supply several copies for re-takes.

Sets are constructed from the Drafts-men's plans by teams of craftsmen and women—carpenters, plasterers, painters, paperhangers, welders, plumbers, etc. For sets on location, the Art Director accompanies the Director on the inspection tour of sites. His eye will spot details out of context which cannot be disguised. Art work must be accurate in every detail however small; the Director may want to use it in close-up.

Left. A major set under construction on "E" Stage, Pinewood Studios, England for *Slipstream* (1989). (Right) One of the public galleries of the Victoria and Albert Museum, London, which was used as a *Slipstream* location.

Below. While many art directors now use the authentic location, sets which require spectacular special effects are custom-built within studios. The largest sound-stage in the world was built specially to accommodate the submarine-base set for *The Spy Who Loved Me* (1977) at Pinewood. Still in use, it is known as Stage "007" after the film character James Bond and the Bond films – which are renowned for sensational sets constructed at considerable expense only to be blown to bits during the shooting of the climactic scene of the action.

# The Director

From the beginning and through all stages of production, the Director of the movie makes the artistic decisions which determine how the story is told. With the Producer, s/he chooses the key members of the Unit for their special talents. S/he then forms a team who will work together to make the movie. The first thing they learn from the Director is how s/he intends to interpret the script. This is explained visually in the storyboard: a layout, in cartoon form, of the screenplay on which the major shots are drawn.

With the storyboard and the first overall pictures in mind, each department now sets to work. While they are gathering together their individual crews, their materials, and their equipment, the Director will, if s/he can, begin to rehearse the principal members of the cast. During this time, as s/he is shaping the narrative line of the film with them, their personalities and performances are helping to fill in the visual lines. If an actor lifts an eloquent eyebrow, for instance, the Director may immediately mark it for a close-up. By the time it comes to shooting, the Director will have the measure of how to break down the script into **set-ups** and single shots.

Technically, a set-up is created each time the camera is moved to accommodate a shot for which the lighting has to be changed. A shot is created when the camera, rolling, is pointed in a certain direction. In a **tracking shot**, a camera on a **dolly** can travel from shot to shot in a single set-up. Camera techniques are the means by which the Director tells the story visually. The manner in which s/he chooses to use them is the artistic "how." During post-production, the Director may re-arrange the story order, delete entire scenes, or add library shots (background shots from other filming).

CLOSE UP

MEDIUM SHOT

MEDIUM LONG SHOT

By selecting a particular shot in relation to the previous one, the director builds each sequence to a chosen climax. To this end, s/he selects from the range of shots which are illustrated. In determining the shot, s/he establishes a narrative point of view: i.e. what is of importance to the action – the subject, the background or a combination of both. Some directors use a director's finder. This is a calibrated instrument like a small telescope with a variable range of view with which to scan the action field. Others rely on an instinctive choice dictated by experience and/or artistic judgment. Often there is a combination of both methods.

# The Actors

David O Selznick's *Gone With The Wind* (1939). The famous scene showing the Confederate Army's wounded at the Atlanta railroad station. Star Vivien Leigh (wearing red dress, left) is seen surrounded by a host of the extra artists who were engaged for this film.

Casting is one of the most crucial operations in the making of a movie. If a director gets it right, it means that half his work is already done. The ideal cast occurs when the actors fit the characters and also interlock with each other like jigsaw pieces in the finished picture.

Casting usually begins with a star. Financial backers prefer the "guarantee" of a famous face. If a popular star is available, willing, and right for the part, the director is most fortunate. With a name to quote, he can now fill the feature and supporting roles.

What is the difference between the two kinds of role? It is a matter of the order in which actors' names appear on the **billing**. Fees are negotiated on the basis of an actor's standing, not by the size of the role, and the billing reflects this. Feature players rank higher than supporting actors, and play the juicier parts.

Further down the cast list are the actors who make short appearances in the small scenes which move the action along and contribute to the vitality of the movie. For these roles, a director will often use the services of a Casting Consultant. Sometimes called Casting Directors, their job is to see the work of every actor and actress around and to file their credits, with comments. When directors send them scripts for casting suggestions, they arrange interviews and readings of the role with him/her.

For the **extra** men and women, the First Assistant contacts the Extra Agencies. Included as members of the cast are the **stunt** men and women and the stunt doubles, the **stand-ins** and the doubles. Animals, their trainers and their handlers are also "cast".

Contracts are negotiated on the number of working days scheduled for each role. A picture-contract is usual for stars and some feature players. This gives the production company exclusive call on the actor for the duration of shooting, regardless of the number of working days. Post-production work is negotiated separately.

Supporting roles usually carry a daily-rate contract. This guarantees a fee for a specified number of days' work within certain dates. Any call on either side of those dates is paid at a rate for each extra day. Extras receive a daily fee.

A star's contract is a personal document. Negotiable clauses include the manner of payment (a "piece of the picture" contract guarantees a shooting fee plus a percentage of all of the takings). Specifications may cover the size of the lettering and the placement of the star's name on the credits, length of exposure time on the screen and the number of close-ups, number of promotional appearances, details of over-all expenses, personal expenses. On the Floor, the star is known as "The Money."

# Costume

Clothes worn on the screen are called "costumes," even if they appear to be only shirt-and-jeans. Every costume has its place in the composition of the frame: the choice of colors and the texture of the fabrics add information. It makes a definite statement about the character who is wearing it. A tramp in a ballroom, for example, is immediately recognized by his clothes.

The Costume Designer starts to work during pre-production, in consultation with the Director, the Production Designer, the Art Director and the leading actors. It is essential for the costumes to be in character and to be comfortable. This must be sorted out before shooting begins. The Floor must never be kept waiting because of costume difficulties.

The costume information chart carries the personal measurements of all players including extras. It also covers the numbers of scenes in which each costume appears and where changes are required. When the action calls for clothes to be broken down—that is, showing varying stages of wear—the effect is created by distressing a series of identical garments which double for the original. The Designer will have a working knowledge of color photography and the effect of lighting on colors and materials. The shades and tones which reflect the mood of the

script are discussed with the Director and also with the Art Director, who must ensure that the costumes neither repeat nor clash with the set furnishings. Specialist costume houses make costumes from original design-drawings. They also rent from their considerable stocks.

During shooting, costumes are in the care of the Wardrobe Department. Male and female dressers are responsible for the condition of everything which is worn during filming, including the laundering. But when, say, sauce has to be splashed on a shirt during a take, if the character moves immediately from an interior to an exterior set, there could be an interval of several weeks before the follow-on scene is shot. The garment is hung on the "Do Not Disturb" continuity rail.

Left. Costume design sketches for the characters Belitski and Tasker in *Slipstream*, drawn by Helen McCabe in the film's Costume Design department. (Below) The costumes as they are worn by Kitty Aldridge (Belitski) and Mark Hamill (Tasker).

# Make-up and Hairdressing

The purpose of make-up is to transform the actor's appearance into that of the character. But sometimes the character seems to look like the actor himself—so why does he need make-up?

During the processing of color photography, each print of the film is defined by the actors' skin tones. So that these can be reproduced accurately during the often disjointed sequences of shooting, cosmetics are used. They ensure continuity of color and appearance. A make-up artist must know about color technology and must also be a bit of a bio-chemist. Skin reactions to the ingredients of the cosmetics vary. And in a cast of, say, thirty actors, each person's skin will react individually.

In the first instance, the Make-up Designer studies the facial features and skin type of the principal actors in the movie. From this, s/he makes experiments.

The cosmetics are numbered and each stage of the operation is charted. The make-up is then tested by the actor in front of the camera. This Make-up and Camera Test is a sort of contest. To score, Make-up must deceive the camera, while the camera must try to seek out any flaws. All traces of the cosmetics must be blended into the skin indiscernibly, in order not to be caught in a **close-up**.

As well as creating appropriate hair styles, the work of the Hairdressing Department includes the design and care of hair-pieces and wigs. This calls for a similar talent for deception. A wig-join is where the hair-line meets the facial skin: it is the lace front of a silk cap into which every single hair has been knotted separately to create the wig. Many stars, male and female, prefer to wear wigs and hair-pieces in front of the cameras. The art of movie hairdressers is to keep it a secret.

During shooting, Make-up and Hairdressing artists start the day around 6am. Their work must be ready for shooting at 8.30am. For the rest of the day they will be in attendance on the floor for re-touching before each take and for any changes that the action calls for. At the end of the day's shooting, Make-up remains to clean up the actors, and Hairdressing to remove make-up from the hair-lace of wigs and to shampoo fixatives from the actors' own hair. First to arrive, last to leave—these departments have a long day.

For a basic camera make-up, a tinted base is applied to the face with a silk sponge. The base is made from either modified grease or impacted powder ("pancake"). Shadings and highlights are smoothed into the base with sable brushes. For a matte finish, which will not reflect the lights, a colorless powder is pressed on lightly. The eyes and mouth are outlined and emphasized with further brushwork. To represent the ageing process, the base is omitted and the shading and highlights are first powdered and then overlaid with liquid latex to simulate skin distortions such as wrinkles. By covering the right or left side of the face in the illustration, it is possible to compare make-up details between the two.

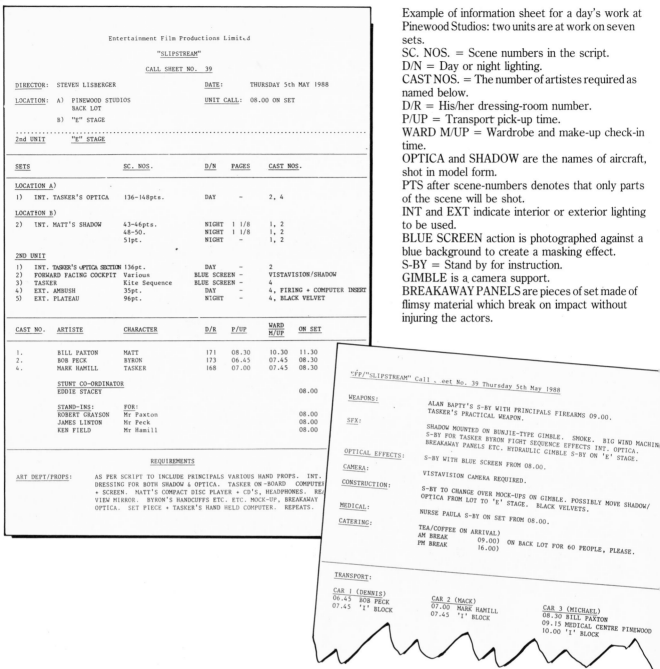

Entertainment Film Productions Limited

"SLIPSTREAM"

CALL SHEET NO. 39

DIRECTOR: STEVEN LISBERGER — DATE: THURSDAY 5th MAY 1988

LOCATION: A) PINEWOOD STUDIOS BACK LOT — UNIT CALL: 08.00 ON SET

B) "E" STAGE

2nd UNIT "E" STAGE

| SETS | SC. NOS. | D/N | PAGES | CAST NOS. |
|---|---|---|---|---|
| LOCATION A) | | | | |
| 1) INT. TASKER'S OPTICA | 136-148pts. | DAY | - | 2, 4 |
| LOCATION B) | | | | |
| 2) INT. MATT'S SHADOW | 43-46pts. | NIGHT | 1 1/8 | 1, 2 |
| | 48-50. | NIGHT | 1 1/8 | 1, 2 |
| | 51pt. | NIGHT | - | 1, 2 |
| 2ND UNIT | | | | |
| 1) INT. TASKER'S OPTICA SECTION | 136pt. | DAY | - | 2 |
| 2) FORWARD FACING COCKPIT | Various | BLUE SCREEN | - | VISTAVISION/SHADOW |
| 3) TASKER | Kite Sequence | BLUE SCREEN | - | 4 |
| 4) EXT. AMBUSH | 35pt. | DAY | - | 4, FIRING + COMPUTER INSERT |
| 5) EXT. PLATEAU | 96pt. | NIGHT | - | 4, BLACK VELVET |

| CAST NO. | ARTISTE | CHARACTER | D/R | P/UP | WARD M/UP | ON SET |
|---|---|---|---|---|---|---|
| 1. | BILL PAXTON | MATT | 171 | 08.30 | 10.30 | 11.30 |
| 2. | BOB PECK | BYRON | 173 | 06.45 | 07.45 | 08.30 |
| 4. | MARK HAMILL | TASKER | 168 | 07.00 | 07.45 | 08.30 |
| | STUNT CO-ORDINATOR EDDIE STACEY | | | | | 08.00 |
| | STAND-INS: | FOR: | | | | |
| | ROBERT GRAYSON | Mr Paxton | | | | 08.00 |
| | JAMES LINTON | Mr Peck | | | | 08.00 |
| | KEN FIELD | Mr Hamill | | | | 08.00 |

REQUIREMENTS

ART DEPT/PROPS: AS PER SCRIPT TO INCLUDE PRINCIPALS VARIOUS HAND PROPS. INT. DRESSING FOR BOTH SHADOW & OPTICA. TASKER ON-BOARD COMPUTEF + SCREEN. MATT'S COMPACT DISC PLAYER + CD'S, HEADPHONES. RE/ VIEW MIRROR. BYRON'S HANDCUFFS ETC. ETC. MOCK-UP, BREAKAWAY OPTICA. SET PIECE + TASKER'S HAND HELD COMPUTER. REPEATS.

EFP/"SLIPSTREAM" Call Sheet No. 39 Thursday 5th May 1988

WEAPONS: ALAN BAPTY'S S-BY WITH PRINCIPALS FIREARMS 09.00. TASKER'S PRACTICAL WEAPON.

SFX: SHADOW MOUNTED ON BUNJIE-TYPE GIMBLE. SMOKE. BIG WIND MACHIN S-BY FOR TASKER BYRON FIGHT SEQUENCE EFFECTS INT. OPTICA. BREAKAWAY PANELS ETC. HYDRAULIC GIMBLE S-BY ON 'E' STAGE.

OPTICAL EFFECTS: S-BY WITH BLUE SCREEN FROM 08.00.

CAMERA: VISTAVISION CAMERA REQUIRED.

CONSTRUCTION: S-BY TO CHANGE OVER MOCK-UPS ON GIMBLE. POSSIBLY MOVE SHADOW/ OPTICA FROM LOT TO 'E' STAGE. BLACK VELVETS.

MEDICAL: NURSE PAULA S-BY ON SET FROM 08.00.

CATERING: TEA/COFFEE ON ARRIVAL)
AM BREAK 09.00) ON BACK LOT FOR 60 PEOPLE, PLEASE.
PM BREAK 16.00)

TRANSPORT:

CAR 1 (DENNIS)
06.45 BOB PECK
07.45 'I' BLOCK

CAR 2 (MACK)
07.00 MARK HAMILL
07.45 'I' BLOCK

CAR 3 (MICHAEL)
08.30 BILL PAXTON
09.15 MEDICAL CENTRE PINEWOOD
10.00 'I' BLOCK

Example of information sheet for a day's work at Pinewood Studios: two units are at work on seven sets.
SC. NOS. = Scene numbers in the script.
D/N = Day or night lighting.
CAST NOS. = The number of artistes required as named below.
D/R = His/her dressing-room number.
P/UP = Transport pick-up time.
WARD M/UP = Wardrobe and make-up check-in time.
OPTICA and SHADOW are the names of aircraft, shot in model form.
PTS after scene-numbers denotes that only parts of the scene will be shot.
INT and EXT indicate interior or exterior lighting to be used.
BLUE SCREEN action is photographed against a blue background to create a masking effect.
S-BY = Stand by for instruction.
GIMBLE is a camera support.
BREAKAWAY PANELS are pieces of set made of flimsy material which break on impact without injuring the actors.

# Production: Shooting

Shooting begins on what is called The First Day of Principal Photography. Let us outline a typical day on a sound-stage, starting at 8.30am.

The first set-up is to be a master shot. This is an establishing shot of the complete scene, to identify the place and all the characters involved in it. It is to be a medium shot (masters are either medium or long shots).

The Director of Photography (DP) and the Director have agreed on the lighting and are rehearsing moves and positions with the actors' stand-ins. The Director looks into the camera to check the angle and notices that an important prop is just out of shot. Adjustments are made to its positioning on the set.

The actors are called to the floor. When they arrive they "walk through" the set to make themselves familiar with the furniture, the hand props, the exits and the entrances.

Next comes the camera rehearsal. This is a **sync-take**, so it includes Sound. Further adjustments. Final rehearsal. Then—ready to go. Make-up, Hairdressing and Wardrobe make their final checks.

*Before every take:* First (Assistant Director) calls "Red light." This light is a signal to everybody, inside and outside the sound-stage, that shooting is in progress. Simultaneously a warning bell is rung. All entrances are closed to ensure absolute silence.

Operator checks every control on his camera. Recordist checks the signal on each channel. First Assistant Director calls "Turn over" and Recordist calls "Speed" when up to the required speed. Camera Operator calls "Rolling" when up to speed. The slate is lifted, the details chalked on it are recorded on camera, and the slate is clapped. Director orders "Action." And the scene is shot. It ends when the Director calls "Cut."

*After every take:* Camera and Sound switch off. Immediate checks are made by the Director with the DP and the Script Supervisor. The Recordist replays the sound tape. If for any reason the quality of the take is unacceptable to any of them, the Director orders "Go again."

**Grips** restore the set. The clapper/loader fills in details of the previous **take** on the Picture Negative Report sheet. The Director informs the clapper/loader if s/he wishes the take to be printed. (Frequently if the Director approves the artistic quality of a take, it is printed and any technical imperfections are removed in the editing.)

At some point during each set-up, the Recordist makes an atmosphere-recording of the **ambient noise** (buzz) as it is during a take. For this, everyone on the Floor, with their equipment, retains their same position. Silence is maintained to reproduce the identical sound level. When all departments are satisfied, the actors leave the set, the lights are switched off, and the line-up begins for the next set-up. The same procedure is repeated each time.

Actor Mark Hamill performs a stunt on the studio back lot (see SET 4 on the information sheet opposite). Eddie Stacey, Stunt

Co-ordinator (wearing red sleeve-band) supervises, watched by Director, Steven Liseberger.

# The Camera

The Director of Photography (DP) is actually the director of the lighting of the film. The Director chooses the positioning of the camera. The DP selects the lamps and orders their positioning, in order to create the mood which the Director wishes. A simple example would be that of shadows. They can be produced to suggest menace or they can be eliminated to give blandness. These changes are called "lighting patterns". The artistry in executing them lies in blending the performance of the lights with that of the camera. Technically, lighting patterns are achieved by the manipulation of machinery and equipment. Using a light filter, the DP calculates the **exposure** which is needed for each shot. In opening or closing the aperture of the camera lens and by choosing a particular filter for an individual lamp, the DP regulates the precise combination between the two.

　　The result is seen, in miniature, through the camera viewfinder. From this, the DP estimates how it will expand to fill the screen.

　　Each set-up has to be lit separately. The lighting for a close-up on a face will differ from that in the master shot, but the effect must be the same. The Camera Operator does not merely start, move, and stop the machinery. His job is to keep the actors in frame wherever they may move on the set. The camera, meanwhile, may also be moving. At the same time as it is tracking forward it could be **panning** from left to right and moving up and down. The Operator has to hold all this activity together in the viewfinder. Meanwhile the Focus-Puller has to keep several other objects on the set in focus. These will probably be positioned at different distances from the camera. Each lens has a different **depth of field**. After the DP has set the aperture of the lens for the shot, the Focus-Puller checks the distances between the camera and the objects, to make sure that each is in focus within the field.

Above. A contemporary electronically controlled camera. It is interesting to compare it with the 1926 hand cranked camera on page 2.

Right. Actor Bob Peck is tied to a giant kite which is in turbulent flight, with actor Bill Paxton moving towards him. (Note the mattress out of shot in case of a free fall.) For this shot, the camera is mounted on a cantilevered boom and is held by the Camera Operator on his right shoulder. This enables him to follow the swaying movements of the action without losing focus. *Slipstream*. A boom shot gives the camera the ability to pan, tilt and to travel in any direction, displaying a versatility undreamed of in the days of the stationary tripod mount.

16

# The Slate

Before each take, the clapper/loader chalks details of it on the slate in order to identify it on film. With camera rolling, the arm on top of the board is lifted and the name of the movie and the number of the take are called. The arm is then clapped down. It is this point, in sound and vision, which the Editor will use to synchronize the image on the film stock with the noise of the clapper on the sound tape. Nowadays, Camera and Sound are also electronically synchronized.

After each take, the clapper/loader makes a written record of the shot by filling in the Picture Negative Report Sheet. Details required for this include the information on the slate plus the camera magazine number with its overall length of stock. Other items include the footage-counter reading, the length of the take (in **footage** and time), the letter P if the take is to be printed and if in color or b/w, whether the scene is day or night, interior or exterior. Takes not to be printed are marked **out-takes**. Four copies are made of each sheet. These are circulated to the Film Laboratories, the Production Office, Camera Department and Accounts Department.

When the clapper/loader takes the footage-counter reading, s/he checks the magazine. This contains the negative film stock inside the camera. A usual magazine length of 35mm film would be 1000ft, which gives ten minutes shooting. Assuming an average of five takes per set-up, around five magazines would be used per day.

Loading and reloading the magazine is a delicate operation. If the film is accidentally exposed to the light, it will be ruined. Confusingly, once it has been used—i.e. images have been photographed on it—it is referred to as exposed film. As such, it is sealed into its can and identified with its slate information. It is then ready for dispatch, with the Negative Report Sheet, to the laboratories as the **dailies**.

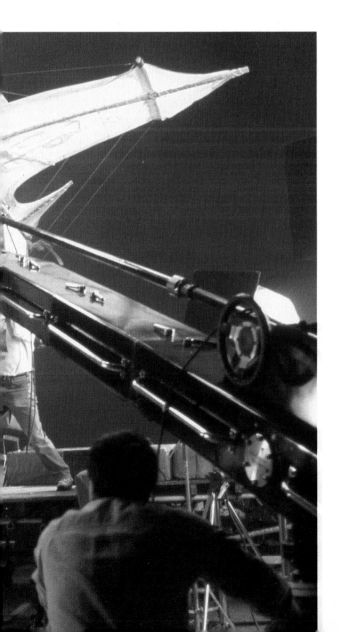

# Lighting

The man in charge of lighting is the Gaffer. He is the head electrician. He reads the script and in consultation with the Director of Photography he draws up the Lighting Plot. From this the Gaffer estimates which equipment will be needed. Checking the Schedule, he orders where and when it will be rigged. Once on the Floor, he, with his Best Boy and the crew, is responsible for producing the lighting effects and any special electrical effects which may be required.

The Gaffer will sometimes advise the DP on the interpretive use of the equipment. After the lamps have been rigged and the general level of lighting for each set-up has been established, the lighting is then adjusted, by various means. For example, all lamps, from "brutes" (the largest) to "babies" (the smallest) have "barn doors." These are square-shaped detachable metal frames. Each side has a moveable flap (the barn door) attached to it. The frame is slotted in front of the face of a lamp. The "doors" can then swing open or shut to regulate the amount of light provided by the lamp. Similarly, a specific effect of a shadow on a wall can be created by a "go-bo." This is a stencil cut-out, which is pinned to the barn doors. Colored acrylic filters attached in the same way make color and tone corrections.

On the sound-stage, cables carry the lighting power from the outlet source to a control-center unit on wheels. This is about the size of a domestic refrigerator, and is the distributor which feeds all of the equipment cables. On location, where the "brutes" are mostly in use, mobile generators provide the source of power. Here, reflectors are also used. They are hand-held by the crew in order to intensify or to mitigate the natural light outdoors. Flat, with rectangular or circular frames, they are colored silver to reflect light, black to absorb light and gold to make it glow.

Ready for location shooting, a 60 KW "load-carrying" mobile alternator is pictured with its contents displayed around and on it. They include incandescent and quartz luminaires, stands, cabling and distribution equipment. (Note the "barn doors.") A sound stage with its own electricity supply can command much more power and equipment.

# Sound

The positioning of the microphone during a tracking shot is resolved by the Recordist in consultation with the Sound Mixer. For this exterior shot, Producer/Director Sir Richard Attenborough is working with the Boom Operator to pick up ambient sound made by the crowd for *Cry Freedom*.

The Sound Mixer is in sole charge of all sound levels throughout the shooting periods. What you actually hear on a movie sound track is a composition of many noises—the voices of the actors, the background ambience, the sound effects and the music—synchronized with the images on the screen. This is achieved by use of "double system". The image is recorded on film, while—separately but simultaneously—the sound is recorded on quarter-inch magnetic tape.

In the near-perfect recording conditions of a sound-stage, the dialog is recorded against the background noises of the studio on a single channel tape. A separate channel is created during shooting to accommodate the sound-only take which records the ambient buzz. This is needed in order to capture the noise of "silence" when "nothing" is happening, and it will be used for matching purposes during editing. A third channel takes the **wild track**. This is a recording made by the Boom Operator with no film rolling. It is composed of dialog only and is recorded on the floor under the same conditions as for the camera take. All personnel and equipment retain the same positions, in order to reproduce the sound balance with precise accuracy.

Film music is either source music or background music. When it is heard by the characters from an identifiable source on screen, such as from a radio, it is source music. This is pre-recorded and played back as part of the action. Background music is heard only by the audience. It is pre-recorded in a sound studio on a separate track or tracks and introduced into the soundtrack during editing.

During shooting, the Boom Operator manipulates the microphone, which is usually suspended from a **fish-pole** above the action. It has an articulated head which enables the operator to pick up directional sound.

On location, because of intrusive and unavoidable background noises, such as that of aircraft passing overhead, dialog is recorded for timing purposes only. It is picked up on concealed microphones or on personal radio microphones. The scene is "post-sinked" (post-synchronized) later in recording studios, where the lines are dubbed on to a separate tape by the artists. Here they are able to monitor their on-screen performance, and in that way are able to ensure perfect **synchronization** with the lip movements.

# Continuity

During pre-production, the first task of the Script Supervisor (Continuity), is to make a rough timing of the screenplay. From this, s/he estimates the length of time it will take to shoot each set-up and sequence. During shooting, the Script Supervisor's prime duty is to make sure that when the film is cut together the action will flow. To this end s/he works closely with the Director.

When a take is called, the Script Supervisor, armed with a stop watch, her/his script, and colored pencils to mark it, positions her/his chair beside the camera. Between the orders "Action" and "Cut," everything that happens during the take is observed and noted. Apart from obvious costume changes, such as an actor removing gloves (from which hand first?) and set changes (a cushion falls from right to left), subtleties of performance are also noted. An example of this would be an unrehearsed pause, or a sigh, in the dialog. To give audible continuity it will have to be repeated in subsequent shots.

Technical details, such as camera-angles and eye-lines, are also noted. For instance, in shooting the reverse angle of a **two-shot**: in order to give the appearance of continuing action, the shot must make visual sense. One actor must be looking to that side of the camera where his counterpart has already been established. Otherwise the character will have apparently leapt from one side of the screen to the other. Since the two angles may not be shot in sequence, it is vital for such information to be logged.

Before and after each take, the Script Supervisor takes a Polaroid photograph of the set as for the take, against which to check the written notes. The notes are then immediately transferred to the Daily Continuity Report. This opens with the identifications of date, film title, names of director and DP; numbers of the set, the camera, and the set-up; whether day or night, mute or sound. To these are added the take numbers, the footage and the length of screen time. The sheet also contains a description of the camera-shot (e.g. hand-held panning shot), the names of the characters involved, all dialog, and the action directions (e.g. character turns clockwise to the door). This is followed by the observations as noted.

A further Continuity Sheet carries details of any dialog recorded in wild track, also of the ambient sound recording.

## DAILY CONTINUITY REPORT

Production: SLIPSTREAM  
Cameras & Set Ups: A CAM  
5 : I/60mm  
20'-I0'  
T7 + LG4  
(TAKE I ONLY NO. 4 FOG)

Date: 5.4.88  
Set: EXT. PLAIN  
Time Shot: I ' 05"  
Screentime: 0 . 59"  
Weather: DAWN EXT. –STRONG WIND, SANDSTORM, BRIGHT LIGHT

SCENE NO. 98

SLATE NO. 200 (MUTE)

### ACTION & DIALOGUE

MATT into shot L-R  
thru' dust storm  
crawling along on stomach

TAKE I - Complete but gib up too slow & caught lamp Fog fx poss. too much I.08"

Track along L-R  
with MATT thru' f/g rocks  
as he approaches

TAKE 2 - Complete - good - one more without vermiculite timing of MATT's look up not v.g. I.06"

Continue track back to  
find BYRON's legs in  
frame R.

Stop track as they meet  
& MATT stops  
MATT reaches for BYRON's legs  
& looks up to BYRON

TAKE 3 - Complete but exit not v.g. for cam & poss. see f/g rocks move as MATT touches them I.03"

BYRON helps him up  
Gib up to hold T.2/S  
two figures as  
BYRON pulls MATT X shoulder

TAKE 4 - Complete - good I.03"

Track back again L-R  
with T.2/S  
& let them go out R.

TAKE 5 - Complete but smoke ng P/UP

TAKE 6 - Complete PU - good 0.19" P/UP

TAKE 5 P/UP from MATT's look up  
twds BYRON & track staying low  
holding only on legs & feet  
& let them go R.

Preparing to shoot a scene involving a dust storm. *Slipstream.* The Script Supervisor is seen (left) ready to record details of the take, as illustrated on the Continuity Sheet (above).

From it we learn that the scene was shot without dialog, without sound, in four takes. Takes number 5 and 6 were of a single pick-up shot. All six takes were printed.

f/g = foreground; T.2/S = tight two-shot; P/U = pick-up shot to be inserted during editing; ng = no good.

The Producer/Director and crew of *Cry Freedom* shooting a tracking shot on location in Zimbabwe. Track-laying is a precise skill practised by the Grips, who must ensure a smooth and steady ride for the camera no matter how unfamiliar the terrain may be.

# On Location

Location shooting can take place indoors or out of doors. The decision to work outside the studios may be taken for artistic reasons, in that the authentic location is better suited to the Director's purpose. It may be taken for financial and practical reasons, in that it will save the expense of constructing the set on a sound-stage.

Sometimes the whole film is shot on location. In this case, the entire unit travels. But if principal photography is first being shot in the studios, the Second Unit will make a start on the location work. This will be to film the establishing shots of time and place. It will also include long shots of the actors' doubles, working on the stunts, and any special effects, especially those which involve the use of animals. For these set-ups, matching close-ups and medium shots of the principal actors will be taken when the unit joins the location.

In charge of the operation is the Location Manager. It is her/his responsibility first to scout for suitable sites from which the Director may make a choice. S/He then negotiates permissions to use the real estate, and is responsible for the attendant paper-work involved. S/He prepares the property for the unit's use and draws maps for the massive transport undertaking.

Location transportation includes:
camera car, for camera and equipment; lighting truck, for lamps and equipment; electricity generators; sound truck for all sound equipment; make-up and hairdressing trailers with dressing tables, lights and plumbing; wardrobe department van with equipment; principal actors' portable dressing rooms; coach for extra artists; catering truck; dining bus; First Aid van; unit cars for supplying communications back to base, transporting actors and rushing the dailies to and from the labs; honey wagons (toilets).

If animals are to be used, their special transport must also be accommodated.

# Post-production: Processing

When the sealed camera negative arrives at the film laboratories immediately after shooting, it is treated with clinical care. It would be an extremely costly operation to replace it. The first step in processing the film is to develop the negative. From this, the work print, known as the dailies is made.

The dailies are usually **processed** in the laboratories for viewing the following day. This is done in case a scene has to be re-shot—hence the alternative name of **rushes**. Before they are printed, the dailies are machine-cleaned to erase specks of dust. Each negative is then placed in storage, at an even temperature. At this stage, the print has no sound. The sound tapes are transferred on to 35mm tape and are used in synchronization separately.

At the viewing the following day, the Editor and the Director decide which takes are to be selected for the **Cutting Copy**. (In shooting, of the 100,000 feet of negative used, only about 10,000-13,000 feet will be used in making the final cutting copy. The remainder will be stored—never thrown away—in case it is required for future use. Unused sections are either "out-takes," or "trims," i.e. remainders of scenes which have been used.)

While processing continues on the dailies, each day's cutting copy is being edited into shape in the film company's editing room. When it emerges as the Cutting Copy, the picture is sent back to the laboratory for the addition of titles and any special effects, including opticals such as **dissolves**, which will provide a pleasing finish or will indicate the Director's feel for a particular atmosphere.

The original camera negative is then taken out of storage and it is cut to match the Cutting Copy. This is known as the Original Cut Negative. It is carefully color-graded by the Laboratory grader/timer to accommodate the individual lighting of each scene. The process determines the amounts of red, green and blue **additive light** to be used by the printing machine, in order to produce a first trial print which will give continuity of color on the screen. This print is made from the **action cut** negative and the separate **optical sound track** negative.

The laboratory print is the first to bring together the work of the Picture Editor and the Sound Editor. It is screened so that the Director may discuss the final color adjustments with the color-grader, in order to provide a final **answer print**, or show print.

After this work, the Original Cut Negative is cleaned again and from it a master **interpositive** copy is made. The Negative is then returned to storage, where it will be held by the lab for posterity. The Original Cut Negative is the most valuable item of film production: the less it is handled, the less likelihood there is of its being damaged. It is from the master interpositive copy that the duplicates are made for release printing.

The color-grader at work using an analyzer machine. By the adjustment of red, green and blue tones, a color balance is achieved in sympathy with the Director's requirements. For example: to indicate a scene in flashback, sometimes the sepia tones of photography-in-the-past are chosen. Thus, with color technology and individual artistry the grader can create a feeling of mood, time and place.

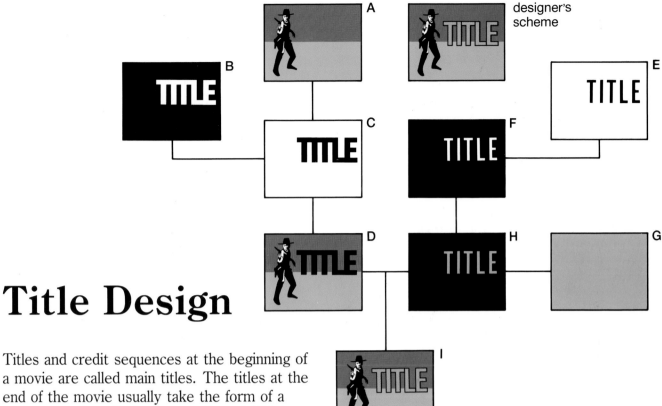

designer's scheme

# Title Design

Titles and credit sequences at the beginning of a movie are called main titles. The titles at the end of the movie usually take the form of a moving list of credits known as a "crawl." Main and end titles are created by a Title Designer.

There are two ways of presenting the main titles. One is to use a quote from the action of the script. With this method, special sequences are written and shot during production, and the title lettering is superimposed on the live-action background. Work on the design can start as soon as the special sequences have been shot.

The second method is for the Designer to see the rough cut when shooting is completed. From this, s/he will perceive the "feeling" of the film. A sequence is then designed from an "abstract" idea of it.

If the first method is used, the Editor supplies cutting copy, with separate sound track, indicating where the titles should be placed in relation to the action and the sound. The Designer provides the title style and also the layouts. In these, s/he places the information in the **field areas** where faces are not obscured. S/he also works with the music arranger to avoid over-emphasis of information: for example, a loud "sting" after an actor's name.

When the designs have been given the approval of the Director and the Producer, they are sent to the Technical Manager of an Optical House. Here the artwork for lettering and of backgrounds is executed. The size of the lettering will depend upon various factors: on the length of the information to be given, for example. If the title is a long one, the letters will

**A** Art work specially created for use as background.
**B** Block of the title's lettering shot on the rostrum camera using high contrast film stock.
**C** Rostrum camera negative used as a matte to run with A.
**D** A and C are photographed together on the optical camera. This process exposes the background but masks the light from the lettering. D is referred to as the *first exposure*.
**E** Separated lettering is shot on the rostrum camera on to high contrast negative stock, as in B.
**F** Rostrum camera negative used to run with G.
**G** Colored filter for lettering color.
**H** The negative stock of the first exposure (D) is run through the optical camera for a second time, exposing the title face (F) and the color filter (G). This exposes the title color into the black area left by process D. As the art work in B is smaller than that in E, when D, H and G are married-up the letters will have a black outline.
**I** The scheme (A) with the completed title superimposed, ready to be cut into the film.

be smaller. There may also be clauses in the stars' contracts which stipulate the percentage of space which their names will fill in relation to the title of the movie.

The title components are first shot by a **rostrum camera**. The negatives are then placed in alignment with a negative of the background film, in an **optical printer**. The two are then shot. This procedure marries the two sequences. When each of the married-up sections have been cut together, the final title negative is attached to the final cut of the movie and they are sent to the lab to be printed.

# Editing

The Editor is responsible for bringing together all aspects of the work during the production and post-production periods. Editing is carried out in specialist cutting rooms. It begins with the assembling of the first Rough Cut. As the dailies begin to arrive from the laboratories, the Editor cuts the sections together in story order—as nearly as s/he can, remembering that scenes have been shot out of sequence. When shooting is completed, the Rough Cut offers the first sight of the movie as a whole. From it, the Director and the Editor work towards the second and third cuts.

The editors use either a flatbed or a Moviola machine. Each machine displays a footage-counter—which measures the length of film stock and the number of frames—and a time-in-seconds counter. Both machines do the same job. The Moviola stands upright. The flatbed—as its name implies—forms a table. Both machines have viewing screens. Once a reel of film has been threaded into either machine it can be moved forwards and backwards and can be stopped at speed. This allows the Editor to mark individual frames with a grease pencil to within fractions of a second.

Gradually the cuts are put together into the second cut, with the positioning of close-ups, medium shots, deletions and transpositions. At this stage the running order of shots can still be changed. After seeing one, or maybe two, further versions, the Producer and the Director are satisfied that the story works and is at the desired length. It is this version which becomes the Final Cut.

The next stage of editing begins with the adding of the **optical** effects. These are the further **fades**, **wipes**, dissolves etc., with which the Director has decided to link the scenes. Also added are any optical effects which occur during the narrative and the main and end titles. The negative of this additional photography is sent to the laboratories for processing and printing. It is then returned to the Editor. S/he then **splices** it into the Final Cut. The movie is now considered to be **locked**.

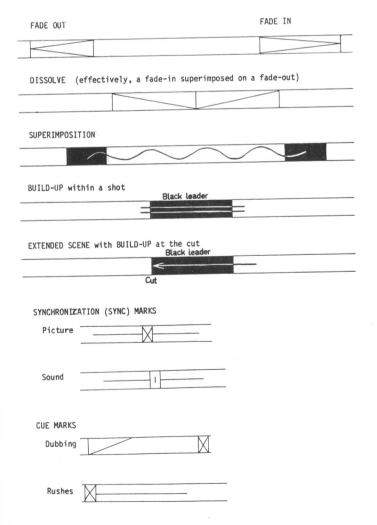

Above. Editor using Moviola machine. The sound track is on the spool, left. The picture is on the spool, right.

FADE OUT                    FADE IN

DISSOLVE (effectively, a fade-in superimposed on a fade-out)

SUPERIMPOSITION

BUILD-UP within a shot
                    Black leader

EXTENDED SCENE with BUILD-UP at the cut
                    Black leader
                    Cut

SYNCHRONIZATION (SYNC) MARKS
    Picture
    Sound

CUE MARKS
    Dubbing
    Rushes

Editor's mark sheet, with examples. Edge numbers are printed on the edges of both film and sound tracks so that all relevant material can easily be related during the matching of negatives.

In magnetic recording a strip of film is coated with minute particles of iron oxide. When it is passed over a magnetic sound head, the modulations are converted into sound. This is transferred to magnetic tape and impressed alongside the picture in synchronization. (Right) A composite photographic impression of the process.

# Sound Editing

A movie's **soundtrack** is an amalgamation of all the sound tapes which have been recorded separately. The three principal ones contain (a) the dialog, (b) the sound effects, (c) the music.

Once the Editor has completed the Final Cut, the Sound Editor "strips" the sound tracks. First s/he isolates the dialog. The next step is to remove any words and noises which, after cutting, no longer relate to the visual image which remains. S/he then fills in the gaps with room tone taken from the relevant soundtrack previously recorded during shooting. This process is known as "cleaning the track." Simultaneously, the Effects Editor will create the effects tracks.

S/he first notes which of the production effects, as they were recorded during shooting, are acceptable. To them the Director may wish to add to or lower the volume for a more dramatic effect, or to replace one sound with another. The Effects Editor adds dimension and sound-color to the action by easing in background sounds. For instance, a woman in a room is silently reading. During shooting, the set was silent, the scene was dead. In the movie it is full of life—clock ticking, distant traffic, dog barking, wind blowing, logs crackling. Each of these sounds is on a separate tape. On his/her copy of the final cut the Effects Editor marks where each noise is required. The effects tracks are then mixed together on to one track.

The Music Composer views the Final Cut. S/he marks (a) where each unit of music, known as a "cue," is to be used and (b) the sound that it should make. S/he then calculates a timing breakdown of each cue with a stop watch. From earlier jottings made during production, the Composer completes the writing of the score. This is recorded in a sound studio. The track is then edited into the picture by the Music Editor. The three principal sound tracks are now ready for the **mix**.

During the mix, each track will have equalization and blending modifications built into it. When all the tracks are played back simultaneously they will sound like a single integrated track. Translated into an **optical signal**, the single track is then *printed* along one side of the film. If sound has been recorded magnetically, the track is *bonded* to the film. The soundtrack is now ready to be lined up in synchronization with the Original Cut Negative. This completes the editing work and the result is known as the **Fine Cut**.

Sometimes it is necessary to "dub" a film into a foreign language. First, the spoken dialog is translated. Next, the script is matched, for sense and vision, with the screen image of the words. Then, in the recording studios, actors watching the screen commit the translated version to a separate dialog tape, ready for editing.

# Special Effects

There are basically two kinds of Special Effects (SFX): Production Effects and Optical Effects. **Production Effects.** These are created during shooting, as part of the action, on the set. Each department displays its own techniques. For instance, the camera can produce slow motion. The standard speed-rate of photography and projection is 24 frames per second. When the camera runs at a faster speed and the film is projected at normal speed, the action appears slower. Conversely, if fast motion is required, the shooting speed is slower. In all departments each effect is rehearsed until the mechanics and the materials used can be produced for as many takes as may be required on the set.

**Optical Effects.** Known as opticals, these are created in the laboratories, design studios and editorial cutting rooms of an Optical House where also there are studios for the **stills** cameras, special effects cameras, rostrum cameras and optical printers.

The technique usually adopted for the creation of opticals is that of "stop motion" or frame-by-frame photography. The standard number of frames per second can be photographed over an unspecified length of time, allowing each picture to be manipulated separately.

Before photography, the SFX Designer will have made a series of **key drawings**. Each of the component parts is then created individually in a separate drawing. The drawings are photographed by the rostrum camera to obtain negative **mattes** which are then placed in alignment on the optical printer. This process controls the areas of exposure and non-exposure. In masking certain areas and revealing others, the optical printer combines component parts from separate images within a single frame.

Optical sequences may contain around 1,000 frames per second, and this painstaking method allows the apparatus to be used creatively as well as mechanically: the effects being composed as the photography progresses.

Models and backgrounds are created in the special effects studios, for use in the final photography of the actual scene.

The techniques employed in creating effects are as diverse as the ingenuity of the designers.

*Front Projection*   Projector throws images on to semi-transparent mirror. Camera lens is pointed through mirror at a highly reflective screen which contains background scene. Screen returns projected image to the camera, which photographs background and foreground in a single operation. Camera and projector are aligned so that the shadow of the foreground subject is exactly behind itself and is unseen by the camera.

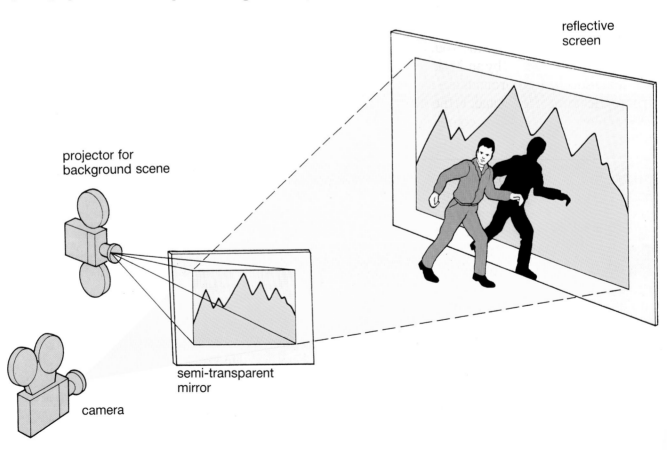

reflective screen

projector for background scene

semi-transparent mirror

camera

# Animation

There are three kinds of animation: (1) Drawn animation, which is created by filming a succession of still drawings; (2) Model or stop-frame animation, produced by filming a model in a succession of poses; (3) Computer animation, in which images are generated and moved by computer on video.

Traditional drawn animation begins with a script and a storyboard which illustrates each scene of the action. A budget breakdown and a production schedule are produced to cost and plan timings for the film—an average 30 seconds' screen time entails about 12 weeks' work.

The Designer creates the style of the film in a series of **key frames**. From these the Director works to develop individual characteristics for the subjects of the film. A sound track of music and dialog is recorded. The Editor breaks down the dialog, first into single words and then into individual sounds. These are charted on **bar sheets**.

From the bar sheets, the Director plans the shooting of the **Leica reel**. The Leica is effectively a filmed storyboard, which is shot to the timings given on the bar sheets, with a drawing to indicate each of the important scenes and positions of the film.

Following the information given on the Leica reel, the Animator draws the rough animation, on paper. S/he is helped by an Assistant and an **In-betweener**. Backgrounds are commissioned from a background artist and, in the Ink and Paint Department, various color combinations are tested.

The **Pencil Test**, or Line Test, is shot using the rough drawings of this first stage of animation, which shows the movement that will be in the final film. After the Pencil Test, the drawings are cleaned by the animation team then passed to the Ink and Paint Department, to be transferred from paper to cel. A cel is a sheet of clear acetate—and as it is easily marked, the artists wear cotton gloves. The drawings are transferred by hand-tracing, or by photocopying, on to the top surface of the cel.

Paint is applied to the back of the cel, the darkest colors first. Sufficient quantities of each color are mixed before painting begins, to ensure a correct match throughout production.

When the background is finished and the

Protected by transparent coating and ready for photography, a collection of "levels" are positioned for assembling a single frame. To ensure precise positioning, the cels are held in alignment by pegs above and below.

cels are painted—sometimes several levels, or layers, of cel for each scene—the Checker makes sure that all artwork is correct before it is sent to camera. S/he has the guidelines of a **dope sheet (exposure sheet)**, on which the Director or Animator has written detailed scene-by-scene instructions for the cameraman. The artwork is shot on a rostrum camera. The film is sent to the labs for developing and printing. When the print is synchronized with the sound track (as separate elements) it is called an **Interlock** or **Doublehead**.

Post Production is the same as for **Live Action**. Sound effects are added, and mixed with the voice tracks at a dubbing session. When picture and sound have both been approved, the negative is cut and the two elements are combined to form the Answer Print.

(Above) The story outline with its complementary stills from the Key Set of promotional material for *Time Bandits*. (Right) The movie's single sheet poster (30 ins × 40 ins) gives the accredited names of its principal creators and illustrates the fantasy nature of the film. Unusually, the poster was designed by the movie's Producer/Director. Examples of poster art have become collectors' items. Many of the finest works of the past can be found in museums.

# Promotion and Distribution

The distribution company is sometimes a movie's principal financial backer. A sum of money is paid in advance to the Producer in exchange for the right to distribute the completed product plus a share in the profits. The company is responsible for the advertising campaign which will promote the movie. Distribution and Advertising are the most expensive items in the cost of making a movie. They account for roughly two-thirds of the entire budget.

Information for promotional material is gathered and put together by the Unit Publicist during shooting. The **Stills Photographer** takes publicity portraits of the actors on and off the sets, and of the action on each set. S/he also makes a photographic record of each working day.

The Publicity Assistant captions all stills with accurate identifications. A selection from the stills is made to promote sales of the movie.

A **key set** is prepared by the distributing companies for press circulation. This consists of a folder containing a number of picture stills and stars' portraits; also a handbook of production information. The latter gives a complete list of credits, a short history of the making of the movie, and biographies of the principal participants.

This information is circulated before and during the three major promotional occasions: the Trade Show, the Press Show and the Première. The first two are generally for daytime attendance. The Trade performance is viewed by Exhibitors and other distribution companies who have exhibiting rights. The Press showing invites film critics, reviewers and gossip writers among other journalists from the media, for their opinions. The Première is often in the evening, and if it is to be a gala occasion it is held in aid of a charitable trust.

# Screens and Projection

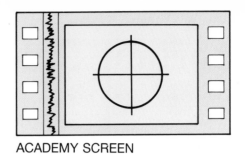

ACADEMY SCREEN

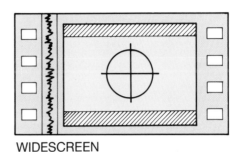

WIDESCREEN

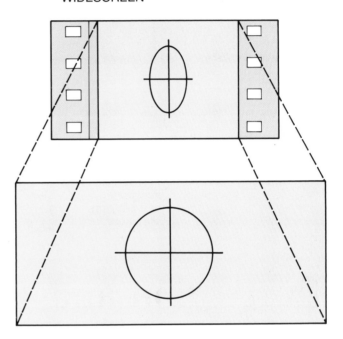

The principle of projection has changed very little since pictures were first transmitted on to a screen. It is mainly the shapes of the screen and the range of the film stock which have altered. Some movies are made on 70mm and on 16mm, but most are still being shot on 35mm film.

Because the dimensions of movie theaters—and therefore the sizes of their screens—differ with each building, the shape of the screen is determined by ratio. The **aspect ratio**, as it is known, represents the shape of the screen as it is viewed by moviegoers. It is calculated by relating the height of the screen, which is known as "1" to its width. Thus a ratio of 2:1 means that the width is twice the height.

The three main screen sizes found in present-day cinemas are:

**1** The original square screen, which is the smallest. Known as "academy" size, it was in general use until the 1950s. At this time, widescreen techniques were adopted by production companies in an effort to combat the growing popularity of small-screen television.

**2** Widescreen, which is the most popular size now in use. The academy size aperture can be masked, above and below, to accommodate the widescreen aspect ratios. Thus it allows the cinemas to run both systems and in each case to use traditional lenses.

**3** Cinemascope or Panavision. These screens show movies which have been shot with a special camera lens. Invented in 1916 by a French optician, Henri Chrétien, the **wide-angle lens** squeezes the image to half its normal width on to the standard 35mm negative. The process is reversed in the projection of the print, when the images are "unsqueezed" and revert to their normal proportions.

To achieve perfect reproduction on the screen, film is fed into a projector which is equipped with a lens. Travelling at the standard speed (24 frames per second) the film passes in front of rays of light. As it does so, the lens focuses the rays and resolves the image of the film, projecting it on to the screen, and magnifying each frame to the size of the screen. Three calculations are necessary to determine the projector lens for screening: (1) the size of the frame of the film; (2) the aspect ratio of the preferred screen size; (3) the "throw," which is the distance between the projector and the screen.

For Cinerama, which had only a short life, three screens, side by side and curved at either end, were needed, as the movies were shot with three separate cameras. The resulting three films had to be projected in synchronization to maintain the illusion of a single panoramic picture. 3D (three dimensional) film was shot with two cameras, and to achieve synchronized vision—it had to be watched through Polaroid spectacles. With the IMAX system, film is projected horizontally. Shot on 70mm film, the pictures are printed lengthways. They are projected (by special projector) on to a curved screen measuring 70ft by 135ft.

# Important Dates

**1877**  E. Muybridge experiments with multiple shutter photography, USA.

**1884**  First celluloid roll film produced by G. Eastman, USA.

**1888**  Camera-Projector with multiple lenses devised by W. Friese-Green, England.

**1889**  First identified American moving film, *Figure With Hand on Horse*. Thomas A. Edison & G. Eastman, USA.

**1893**  First movie exhibition by Edison's Kinetoscope, USA.

First movie manufacturing studio, Kinetographic Theatre, USA.

**1895**  First clear images projected on to a screen, by Robert Paul in England and by Woodville Latham in USA.

Auguste & Louis Lumière patent their invention of the claw device for film projection, France.

**1896**  First cinema built: The Phonographic and Vitascope Parlor, USA.

First fantasy films using trick photography produced by Georges Méliès, France.

**1897**  First Asiatic films produced: by H.S. Bhatvadekar, India and by Shozo Makino, Japan.

**1900**  First use in film-making of inter-cutting technique, *The Life of an American Fireman*, Edwin S. Porter, USA.

First use of color film, tinted by hand, Paris Exhibition, France.

**1903**  First story-drama, *The Great Train Robbery*, E.S. Porter, USA.

Invention of the audion tube for film with sound (phonofilm) by Lee de Forest, USA.

**1908**  First animated cartoon story, *Fantasmagorie*, by Emil Cohl, France.

**1909**  First "western," made by Al Christie in New Jersey, USA.

Carl Laemmle introduces the star system with his IMP Company of contracted players.

**1911**  First Hollywood studio, built by David Horsley on Sunset Boulevard.

**1913**  First "gangster" film, *Fantômas*, Louis Feuillade, France.

**1914**  First "screen spectacular," introducing innovatory camera-movement techniques, *Cabiria*, Giovanni Pastrone, Italy.

First feature-length comedy, *Tillie's Punctured Romance*, written directed and performed by Charles Chaplin, USA.

**1915**  First American full-length feature film, *Birth of a Nation*, D.W. Griffith, USA.

**1919**  First "horror" movie—the Expressionist film *The Cabinet of Dr Caligari*, Germany.

**1925**  *The Battleship Potemkin*, influential film by Sergei M. Eisenstein, Russia.

First successful 3-color additive system perfected by Louis Dufay, patented as Dufaycolor, USA.

**1927**  First commercial use of three-screen three-camera (polyvision) technique, *Napoleon*, by Abel Gance, France.

First films with synchronized sound: (1) newsreel, Movietone Fox; (2) *The Jazz Singer* (part silent) using music; (3) all-talking *The Lights of New York*, USA.

Foundation of the Academy of Motion Pictures, Arts and Sciences, Hollywood, USA.

**1928**  First Mickey Mouse, *Plane Crazy*, (silent), Walt Disney, USA.

**1929**  Mickey Mouse with sound, *Steamboat Willie*, Walt Disney, USA.

**1931**  First successful 3-color subtractive system, patented as "Technicolor," USA.

**1932**  First use of Technicolor: *Flowers and Trees*, Walt Disney, USA.

**1935**  First full-length feature in Technicolor: *Becky Sharp*, Rouben Mamoulian, USA.

**1938**  First full-length animated film, *Snow White and the Seven Dwarfs*, Walt Disney, USA.

**1941**  First feature-length use of stereophonic sound, *Fantasia*, Walt Disney, USA.

**1948**  Break-up of Hollywood studio star contract system. Foundation of independent production companies.

**1952**  Polyvision techniques refined into "Cinerama," USA.

**1953**  First exhibition of 3D film and Cinemascope and wide-screen techniques, USA.

**1956**  Introduction of 70mm film stock, USA.

**1976**  IMAX system devised, Canada.

**1982**  The invention of the Megaspool by Rank Film Laboratories, England, received an American Academy Award (Oscar).

**1987**  Introduction of the 60,000ft Megaspooler and Automatic Unloader by Rank Film Laboratories; acknowledged by a second American Academy Award, England.

# Glossary

**Action cut copy**  *See* Cutting Copy.

**Additive light**  In processing, the correction of constituent elements in the 3-color system of color photography.

**Ambient sound**  Background noise on the set during a take.

**Animation**  A succession of still drawings or poses by inanimate objects which, when photographed in sequence, create the illusion of movement.

**Aspect ratio**  Measurement of the screen assessed by its height in relation to its width.

**Answer print**  The first married print (sound and picture). It is used for checking grading and synchronization.

**Bar sheet**  In animation a chart upon which phonetic sounds are noted in relation to the length of time and the shape of the (character's) mouth required to utter them.

**Billing**  A list of performers in order of appearance.

**Black leader**  *See* Leader.

**Build-up**  Black leader inserted in the cutting copy to indicate missing frames. *See* Leader.

**Close-up**  A shot taken by the camera when it is closest to its subject.

**CRI (Color Reversal Intermediate)**  A single-strand 16mm printing negative composed of sections taken from the original camera negative.

**Cutting copy**  Film (and sound if synchronized) in process of being edited. Also known as action cut copy.

**Dailies**  Film footage rushed through the laboratories for showing the following day, hence their alternative name "rushes."

**Depth of field**  *See* Field.

**Dissolve**  Laboratory process—simultaneous fade-in/fade-out, whereby one shot disappears as another appears.

**Dolly**  A wheeled camera platform. "Dolly in" or "dolly back" brings the camera closer to or further from the subject.

**Dope sheet**  *See* Exposure sheet.

**Doublehead**  *See* Interlock.

**Exposure**  The process of submitting photosensitive material (film) to light.

**Exposure sheet**  In animation, a chart containing the analysis of shooting requirements.

**Extra**  An actor whose role carries no dialog.

**Fade, fade out**  Laboratory process during which the images disappear to black.

**Field**  The perspective. Field area refers to the dimensions of the frame. Depth of field is the range of focus. Field of vision is the area visible in frame.

**Final cut**  1. An editor's workprint before sound is added. 2. A sound editor's last workprint before the sound is mixed.

**Fine cut**  The final working print.

**Fish-pole**  A hand-held rod from which the microphone is suspended, with a reel to adjust the length of cable.

**Footage**  Measurement of a spool of film.

**Go-fer**  An assistant who is usually sent on errands—"go for this, go for that."

**Grip**  A member of a crew whose job it is to grip and haul the items and equipment of his department.

**Interlock**  In animation, the bringing together of pictures and soundtrack. Also known as doublehead.

**In-betweener**  In animation, the artist who draws the linking frames between the subjects' key positions.

**Interpositive negative**  The negative of the interpositive copy which has been taken from the Original Cut Negative. From this, all succeeding copies are made.

**Jump cut**  The effect caused by removing frames within a shot.

**Key drawings**.  Outlines of the methods proposed to achieve special optical effects.

**Key frame**  In animation, the prototype images of characters and of the story.

**Key set**  Publicity photographs taken to promote a film.

**Leader**  Blank film at the head and tail of reels. Black leader is processed unexposed film.

**Leica reel**  The process, in animated film-making, during which the storyboard is filmed with pre-recorded dialog in order to assess the artwork which will be required.

**Live action**  Scenes involving subjects which are shot by a movie camera at or around the rate of 24 frames per second.

**Locked film**  A "locked" film is the final stage of picture editing before the soundtrack is added.

**Married print**  *See* Answer print.

**Matte**  A device or process used for masking part of a frame during photography or printing.

**Microphonic sound**  The vibration of sound waves picked up by a microphone and converted into electric currents for amplification and reproduction.

**Mix**  To combine various sources of sound in a single recording.

**Negative**  Undeveloped film which on exposure to light records the images in reversal: e.g. black appears white.

**Optical**  A device, other than a cut, for changing from one scene to another, or a special effect.

**Optical negative**  The negative of the optical soundtrack.

**Optical printer**  The camera which is used for duplication of film and for the creation of optical effects including titles.

**Optical signal**  The system of sound reproduction when a fluctuating light passes over a photoelectric cell and is then converted into a visible track on film.

**Optical track**  The photographically reproduced soundtrack.

**Option**  A contract between the owner and the buyer of material which, for a fee, grants exclusive rights for a stated use within a stipulated length of time.

**Out-takes**  Sections of a film which remain unprocessed, i.e. unused.

**Panning**  A lateral or vertical movement of the camera.

**Pencil test**  First screening of the Animators' drawings in outline.

**Positive**  The print made from a negative.

**Processing**  Laboratory work on exposed film negatives and on printed copies.

**Rostrum camera**  Used in stop-frame photography from a fixed position.

**Rushes**  *See* dailies.

**Set-up**  A scene or part of a scene which is shot as a single take.

**Shooting**  Filming.

**Shots**  Photographs.

**Soundtrack**  The soundtrack is a line of varying width within a darkened stripe which is placed along one side of the ribbon of film. When light is shone through it, the varying intensities of light cause sounds to be emitted which match the accompanying pictures.

**Splice**  To join film or tape.

**Stand-in**  A person who physically resembles a principal actor and is used for camera rehearsals.

**Stills**  *See* Key Set.

**Stock film**  Unexposed film material; also known as raw stock.

**Stunt**  An act of daring or skill which requires a specialist performer.

**Synchronization**  When the sound track and the picture start and finish at the same point, they are said to be synchronized, or "in sync" (pronounced "sink").

**Sync take**  A shot taken by camera and sound simultaneously.

**Take**  A single run of the camera during shooting.

**Tracking shot**  The camera follows the movements of the performer, along its axis or on specially laid tracks.

**Unit**  The combined film crews and personnel.

**Unit call**  Schedule of events issued to all personnel.

**Wide-angle lens**  Lens with a short focal length and a viewing angle of more than 45 degrees.

**Wild track**  A sound track recording without vision.

**Wild walls**  Sections of flat scenery, usually hinged, which open to admit the camera.

**Wipe**  A laboratory process during which the image of a scene appears to be wiped out by that of the following one.

# Index

# Acknowledgments

Threshold Books and the publishers gratefully acknowledge the help given in the production of this book by Gary Kurtz, Executive Producer, Entertainment Film Productions Ltd; General Screen Enterprises Ltd; and Richard Purdum Animation. We would also like to thank the following for their cooperation: Abbey Road Sound Studios, British Academy of Film and Television Arts, British Broadcasting Corporation, British Film Institute, Eon Productions Ltd, Marble Arch Productions Ltd, Rank Film Laboratories Ltd, Samuelson Film Service Ltd, Samuelson Lighting Ltd, and Universal/UIP Distributors.

**Design and illustration credits**
British Film Institute 3; Alexandra Cawdron (make-up)/photo: Geoffrey Drury 13; photo: Frank Connor 21; Danjaq SA, all rights reserved © 1977 *The Spy Who Loved Me* 9 (bottom), © 1981 *For Your Eyes Only* 10; *Gone With The Wind* © 1939 Selznick International Pictures, Inc. Ren. 1967 Metro-Goldwyn-Mayer, Inc. 11; Handmade Films Distribution Ltd 28; a Marble Arch Production distributed by Universal-UIP/photo: Diana Hawkins 19; *La Bohème* © 1926 Metro-Goldwyn-Mayer Corporation. Ren. 1954 Loew's, Inc. 2; photo: John Price, London 25; Richard Purdum Productions/BBC copyright (animation), Liz Friedman (design) 27; Rank Film Laboratories 22, and front cover; Samuelson Film Services Ltd/photo: Geoffrey Drury 16 (top), 17, 24 (top); Samuelson Lighting Ltd 18; stills photography: George Whitear 8, 9 (top), 12/Pinewood Stills Laboratory, 14, 15, 16 (bottom), 20.

Diagrams and drawings: John Hutchinson 26; Coral Mula 5; Eddie Poulton 23, 29.

Picture research: Gwen Cherrell.

**Editorial consultant**
Ian Shand.

Every effort has been made to trace the holders of copyright for some illustrations in this book. If any acknowledgement has been inadvertently omitted, the publishers will make every effort to rectify the omission in future editions.

### How Movies Are Made

Facts On File, Inc.
460 Park Avenue South
New York NY 10016
USA

**Library of Congress Cataloging-in-Publication Data**
Cherrell, Gwen.
  How movies are made/text, Gwen Cherrell; design, Eddie Poulton.
  32 p. 30 × 21 cm. (How it is made).
  Includes index.
  Summary: Explores the process of film production from first script to distribution, covering such aspects as set, directors, actors, make-up, hairdressing, lighting, and editing.
  ISBN 0-8160-2039-6.
  1. Motion pictures—Production and direction—Juvenile literature.
[1. Motion pictures—Production and direction.] I. Poulton, Eddie.
II. Title. III. Series.
PN1994.5.C37   1989
791.43'0232—dc20                                    89-31329 CIP   AC

Facts On File books are available at special discounts when purchased in bulk quantities for businesses, associations, institutions or sales promotion. Please contact the Special Sales Department of our New York office at 212/683-2244 (dial 800/322-8755 except in NY, AK or HI).

General Editor: Barbara Cooper.
Design by Eddie Poulton.
Composition by Rapid Communications Ltd, London, England.
Printed in England by Maclehose & Partners, Portsmouth.

10 9 8 7 6 5 4 3 2 1